HILL & SMITH
A 200 Year History

HILL & SMITH
A 200 Year History

John Olsen

BREWIN BOOKS

BREWIN BOOKS
19 Enfield Ind. Estate,
Redditch,
Worcestershire,
B97 6BY
www.brewinbooks.com

Published by Brewin Books 2024

© Hill & Smith, 2024

All rights reserved. No part of this publication may be reproduced, stored in a retrieval system, or transmitted in any form or by any means, electronic, mechanical, photocopying, recording or otherwise, without the prior permission in writing of the publisher and the copyright owners, or as expressly permitted by law, or under terms agreed with the appropriate reprographics rights organisation. Enquiries concerning reproduction outside the terms stated here should be sent to the publishers at the UK address printed on this page.

The publisher makes no representation, express or implied, with regard to the accuracy of the information contained in this book and cannot accept any legal responsibility for any errors or omissions that may be made.

A CIP catalogue record for this book is available from the British Library.

ISBN: 978-1-85858-770-7

Printed and bound in Great Britain
by TJ Books Ltd.

Contents

Chair's foreword 7

Part 1: A 200 Year History

Born in the Black Country 11
Through two World Wars 14
New ownership, new energy 16
The late 20th century 18
The Grove revolution 21
Building out 25
Turning 200 30

Part 2: Hill & Smith Today

Galvanizing Services
Joseph Ash Galvanizing 37
V&S Galvanizing 42

Engineered Solutions
Bergen Pipe Supports 46
Birtley Group 48
Creative Composites Group 53
Lionweld Kennedy 57
Novia Corporation 59
The Paterson Group 61
V&S Schuler Utilities Group 63

Roads & Security

ATG Access 68

Asset International Structures 72

Barkers Engineering 75

Hill & Smith Inc. 79

Hill & Smith Infrastructure 83

Mallatite 87

National Signal 89

Parking Facilities 91

Prolectric 93

Chair's foreword

I feel very fortunate to be chairing Hill & Smith as it marks its 200th anniversary. Given the passage of time, the extent to which the group has changed since it was founded in 1824 should come as no surprise. What is more remarkable is how some of its essential qualities and values have endured. It has long been a group that has thrived on entrepreneurialism, on agility, and on using innovation to identify and capitalise on growth market opportunities consistent with its core skills.

Today, we are an international group focused on markets that enjoy long-term structural tailwinds: growing populations, urbanisation, climate change, and increasing health and safety regulation. Against the background of those macro trends, in an uncertain world, our purpose is clear: to enable our customers worldwide to create safe and sustainable infrastructure.

I pay tribute to, and thank, all those colleagues who have been part of Hill & Smith's first two centuries, and those who are taking the group forward into its third. I thank our customers around the world for their continued support, and our shareholders for the faith that they place in our business.

Alan Giddins
Executive Chair

Part 1:
A 200 Year History

Born in the Black Country

During the course of the 19th century, the area of the UK now known as the West Midlands was at the heart of the Industrial Revolution. Its skyline dominated by smoking ironworks, foundries and forges, and with rich seams of coal beneath, it became known as the Black Country, a name and heritage that lives on to this day. *The Illustrated London News*, in 1849, painted a dramatic picture of the region's landscape:

> *"In this Black Country, a perpetual twilight reigns during the day, and during the night fires on all sides light up the dark landscape with a fiery glow. The pleasant green of pastures is almost unknown; the streams, in which no fishes swim, are black and unwholesome; the natural dead flat is often broken by high hills of cinders and spoil from the mines; the few trees are stunted and blasted; no birds are to be seen, except a few smoky sparrows; and for miles on miles a black waste spreads around, where furnaces continually smoke, steam engines thud and hiss, and long chains clank, while blind gin horses walk their doleful round".*

It was into this hotbed of industrial activity that Hill & Smith was born when, in 1824, Edward Hill founded Edward Hill & Co. at the Brierley Hill Ironworks. Some years later he introduced into the business his much younger brother-in-law, Henry Smith. When Hill died in 1853, his interest in the business was continued by his wife Emma, alongside her brother Henry, and they changed its name to Hill & Smith.

Between them, Emma and Henry stewarded Hill & Smith as a partnership for over half a century. Their product range was broad. Including, as it did, fencing, hurdles, gates, railway station roofs, footbridges and walkways, crank shafts, piston rods, architectural steelworks, as well as a local galvanizing plant; it was already showing glimpses of the interests that would continue in the business to this day.

They also showed an ability to attract royal clientele, providing many miles of fencing for Queen Victoria's country estates, as well as elaborate ornamental gates for the palace of King Chulalongkorn of Siam (now Thailand). The international appeal of their ornamental metalwork also extended to the gates at the Hong Kong market and at the European Club in Shanghai.

Emma Hill died in 1897, but Henry Smith remained connected to the business until his death in 1906, at the age of 82. He was succeeded by his eldest son, Joseph, but only for three years until he met an untimely death as a result of a collision in his horse-drawn cart on his commute to work. Joseph was the last working owner with any connection to the founders, and the business was converted into a private limited company.

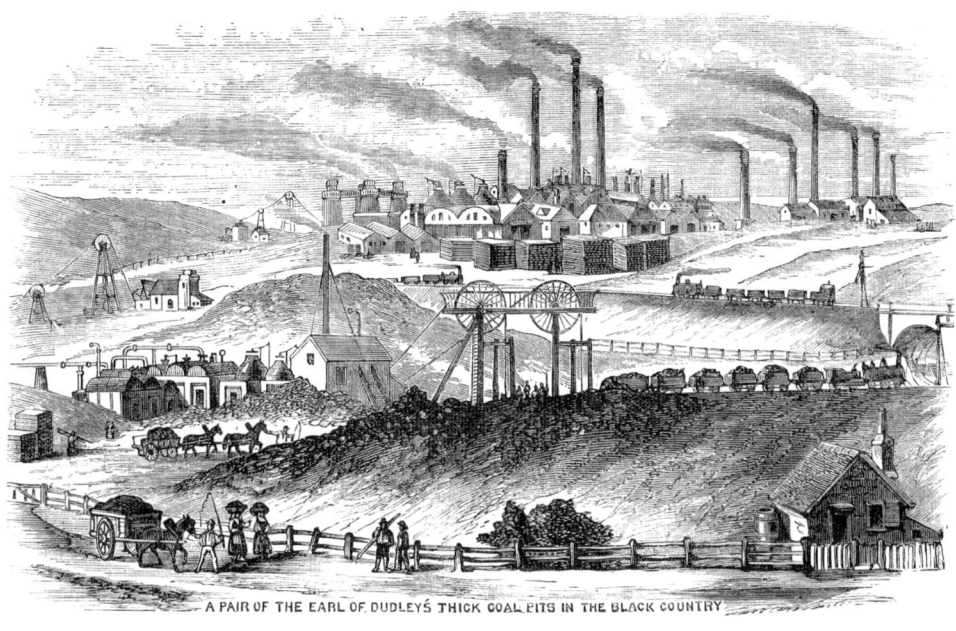

Early 19th century Black Country.

Ornamental gates for the King's palace, Siam, 1900s.

Through two World Wars

In the early years of the 20th century, Hill & Smith was organised into seven departments – fencing; art metal; bridges & roofing; foundry; forge; galvanizing; and rolling mills – manufacturing a wide and eclectic range of products, perhaps demonstrating the early signs of the entrepreneurial culture which has stood the group in such good stead ever since.

Alongside the large decorative ironworks for which they were well known, they were turning out pig troughs, bullock feeding pens, wheelbarrows, stable and saddle-room fittings, shepherds huts, gutters and downpipes, and cast-iron lamp columns. In one year alone, they produced 1,000 such columns for Birmingham Corporation, the local municipal authority. They also continued to make their mark internationally, supplying materials for the British Admiralty's new and expanded naval base in South Africa – the Royal Dockyard at Simon's Town, completed in 1910.

With the onset of the First World War in 1914, production inevitably turned to supporting the war effort. Newly designed iron screw pickets, preferred to traditional wooden posts for supporting barbed-wire defences so that wiring parties, often operating at night, could screw them into the ground without detection, were in high demand and Hill & Smith produced 3.5 million of them during the course of the conflict.

In the all-too-brief inter-war period, the company's focus turned back to steel railings and bridges, including supplying parts of the iconic Sydney Harbour Bridge which opened in 1932. However, with the advent of the Second World War, Hill & Smith's production capacity was again given over to the needs of the government's War Office – air raid shelters, nissen huts (prefabricated corrugated iron structures designed for use as military barracks), parts for the portable Bailey Bridges famously used on D-Day and many other campaigns, rocket firing equipment, parts for landing barges, and cast-iron 'de-gaussing' boxes designed to protect ships from magnetic mines by nullifying the magnetic field created by the ship's steel.

If the industrialisation of the 19th century, and then the two World Wars and the Anglo-German arms race that preceded them, had driven the growth of manufacturing in Hill & Smith's home of the Black Country, the years immediately thereafter proved more challenging. The heavy industry that had shaped the region faded away, and Hill & Smith was not immune. The business soldiered on but the 1950s saw the loss of a number of important contracts and, in the face of an impending crisis, the trustees decided to sell the business in 1960 to a group of prominent West Midlands businessmen – Tom Hampson-Silk, and Leonard and Clive James.

New ownership, new energy

Hampson-Silk and the James brothers set about the dual task of returning the core business to profit and expanding through acquisition. Within two years, their efforts to turn around the loss-making Brierley Hill plant – the site of Edward Hill's original ironworks – had paid off.

Their deal-making ambitions also bore fruit. In 1961, they sealed Hill & Smith's first ever acquisition, with the purchase of a local business, Tipton Steel Stockholders. In 1963, they acquired two closely associated die stamping businesses – Wednesbury Stampings and E Fox Diesinkers.

However, whilst the strategy may have been sound, the new owners were stretched across Hill & Smith and their various other business interests, and the result was that progress stalled. They realised that new blood was needed and in 1964 turned to Denis Hodgetts, an experienced businessman who had earned his spurs at British industrial giant GKN.

The pace of change and growth under Hodgett was impressive. In his first five years, Hill & Smith sold its construction and agricultural interests, leasing to the buyers some 20,000 sq. ft. of spare manufacturing space, and acquired over 2,000 tonnes of drop forging plant and equipment from Westinghouse Brake & Signal, moving it all to the Brierley Hill site. The business then bought the plant, work in progress and order book of Nortons-Tividale, serving both the chemical plant industry and some remaining National Coal Board contracts. It then acquired WH Barker & Son to create the extra capacity needed for the growing flow of orders that the Nortons-Tividale product lines were generating, and finally John Perks & Sons, a supplier of drop forgings, hammers and edge tools.

New ownership, new energy

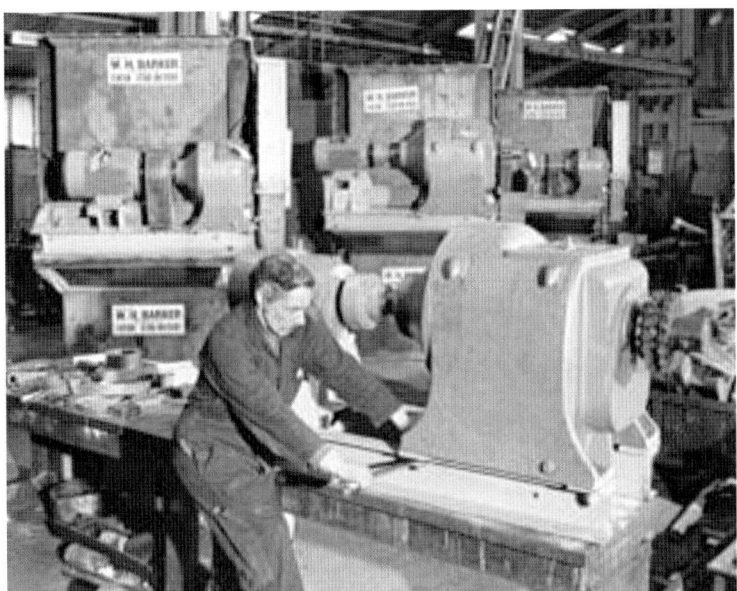

Barkers Engineering 1960s.

A common feature of all these deals was that they involved businesses that were, to a greater or lesser degree, in distress but in which Hodgetts and his colleagues could see potential in terms of what they could add to Hill & Smith. Further evidence, perhaps, of the entrepreneurial and opportunistic ethos that was becoming part of the business' DNA.

In 1969, the now strong, profitable and more broadly-based business made its next major move – joining the ranks of the companies affectionately known as the 'Midlands metal-bashers' on the London Stock Exchange. Hill & Smith started life as a publicly listed company with an initial market value of £600,000 and a new chapter began.

The late 20th century

Whilst there were certainly bright spots, the 1970s, 80s and 90s were not kind to Hill & Smith overall. They were blighted by periods of nationwide industrial unrest in the UK, economic recession, tragedy, and – as it turned out – over-reliance on one of the UK's declining industries: steel.

For the majority of the 1970s, its first decade as a listed company, it demonstrated a resilience that was impressive given the poor industrial climate in which it was operating. Its combination of steel stockholding, steel fabrication, forging and construction businesses produced nine years of unbroken growth, such that profits in 1978 broke the £1m mark for the first time. However, few businesses can defy gravity forever. At the end of the decade, there was widespread industrial action in markets on which it depended, with national strikes contributing to the infamous 'Winter of Discontent' of late 1978/early 1979. These took their toll, and profits slumped.

In 1980 the business was hit hard by the death, in a flying accident in France, of its Chairman and significant shareholder, Tom Hampson-Silk, alongside his wife Ruth. At this point, John Silk, Tom's brother and a respected solicitor, joined the Board and would continue the Silk family's close involvement in the business in various guises (as a Director, then Chairman, Deputy Chairman and, latterly, ex-officio Life President) until his death in 2013 at the age of 89.

In the early 1980s recession meant that the steel industry, on which Hill & Smith depended, was having a torrid time and, to make matters worse, the group was again hit, in 1983, by the unexpected death of one of its leaders – Denis Hodgetts – who had served as Managing Director, and latterly Chairman, for almost 20 years. Roy Skidmore, already a Director, stepped into the role, later to be succeeded by Michael Sara.

In 1982 the group was renamed Hill & Smith Holdings PLC, reflecting the ambitions to broaden out the business. The Board made clear that it was open to acquisitions and, even then, showed its preference for light-touch management from the centre:

> "Many private companies are apprehensive about losing their independence, but our policy is to leave successful management teams to continue operating independently and with guidance rather than interference".

A handful of early deals were done, among them Birtley Manufacturing, Asset Building Components and, in 1986, the £2m purchase of Armco Construction Products. These helped profits bounce back for a few years, edging over the £6m mark in 1988, before recession hit again.

Critically though, the acquisitions – including that of Varley & Gulliver in 1990 – had done little to address the group's over-reliance on the UK steel sector, with the result that the early 1990s were very difficult indeed. The Chairman defended this approach at the time by arguing that:

> "There may be those who would have wished that we had diversified away from steel. However, that is what we are – a steel-based business – it is where our skills lie, and diversification into the unknown can be a recipe for disaster".

Addressing increasingly restless shareholders, and in what can only be described as a heroic attempt to gild the lily, the Board declared, in their report for 1992, that:

> "There is room for some satisfaction since our results compare very favourably with other [similar] groups. Indeed, in 1991 we were the 28th best performing Midlands share".

Those shareholders may, or may not, have been reassured.

By 1997, profits had fallen back to just a little over £1m, close to where they had been 20 years previously, and the group had been hit hard by bad debts from the collapse of at least one major customer. The following year it dropped into loss. David Winterbottom, an accountant with extensive experience of listed company directorship, was brought in as Chairman and he, along with the group's major shareholders, could see clearly that urgent and fundamental change was required. The architect of that change was identified, in the form of David Grove.

The Grove revolution

Too much emphasis can sometimes be placed on an individual's contribution to a company's success. However, it is no exaggeration to describe David Grove as the father of the modern-day Hill & Smith.

Grove joined in 1998, initially as Development Director with a brief to conduct a root-and-branch strategic review, but was rapidly promoted to the role of Chief Executive. He had already carved out a reputation for pragmatic, no-nonsense decision-making in the Midlands business world, not least at the helm of his own group, Grove Industries, which had a diverse portfolio of interests from car parts manufacture and chemicals, to printing and magazine publishing.

What he found on arrival was a group with turnover of almost £80m but making no money, and with its management and resources spread over 15 different profit centres. *"The company was relying too much on history"*, Grove reflected later, and there was certainly no room for sentiment. One of his first steps was to relocate the Hill & Smith manufacturing operations to a purpose-built facility at Bilston, near Wolverhampton, ending a 175-year presence at Brierley Hill, the birthplace of the business.

He also had little time for people who he felt were standing in the way of progress, referring to them as the *"Business Prevention Unit"*. He energetically set about the task of disposing of the loss-makers, streamlining the structure and reporting lines, and focusing the group on areas where it had either a significant market position or a differentiated product offering. It was also at this time, in 1999, that Hill & Smith established its first meaningful overseas manufacturing presence with the establishment of a pipe supports plant (albeit short-lived) in Louisiana, USA, as well as one in Thailand. In the same year, the group acquired

Berry Systems, a UK supplier of off-highway barriers, for £3m – the group's first full acquisition for six years.

But that was just the start. After the initial streamlining, Grove fashioned a quantum leap for the group, with the acquisition in late 2000 of Ash & Lacy PLC, itself listed on the London stock market, for £70m. The deal more than trebled the size of Hill & Smith overnight. With the underperforming Ash & Lacy dwarfing its acquiror in scale, the move was not without risk. The bid was unsolicited, at least as far as the target's management were concerned (their shareholders were all for it). But this was David Grove in his element. He was heard to say to his management teams:

> *"I won't sack you for taking a risk and it going wrong. But I will sack you for doing nothing".*

It was a business with multiple interests, including a sizeable property portfolio, but hidden within Ash & Lacy was one business that, for Hill & Smith, was the jewel: the galvanizing business of Joseph Ash. Adding Joseph Ash to the group's existing galvanizing operations created the foundations for a business that would, over time, be a key contributor to the group.

Whilst the divisional structure went through a number of iterations as the deal flow continued, the overall direction of travel was clear. Grove and his colleagues were intent on creating an entrepreneurial group of businesses focused on product innovation, serving growth sectors, and capable of delivering sustained value to shareholders. Out of this strategy emerged a substantial Infrastructure Products Group, supplying safety barriers, vehicle restraint systems, railings and fencing (through Hill & Smith Ltd, Asset VRS, Berry Systems, Brifen, Varley & Gulliver, and Barkers), flood water storage tanks (Weholite), and street lighting columns (Mallatite). Increased public spending on the UK transport network was to be a major driver of growth.

Road barrier had been on the list of Hill & Smith's activities since 1970, becoming a significant part of the group before the Varley & Gulliver acquisition in 1990 added vehicle containment bridge parapets to the mix. However, it was really from 1999 that the roads-related business started to broaden out in a material way. That year saw the launch of Varioguard, the group's first temporary

The Grove revolution

crash barrier rental solution, that rapidly became the market leader. The acquisitions of Techspan in 2005 and Counters & Accessories in 2006 led to the creation of a technology division within the roads business, providing a range of electronic highway information and vehicle logging and detection systems to complement the more traditional metal-based products.

Alongside the Infrastructure Products Group was the emerging Galvanizing business. The addition of Joseph Ash had resulted in the group commanding over 25% of the UK market, so it is little surprise that eyes turned to opportunities for expansion further afield. In 2005, Grove engineered his second major deal that would, over time, transform the future shape of Hill & Smith: the acquisition of a 33% interest in Zinkinvent GmbH. Zinkinvent, a German investment company, owned a galvanizing and electrical substation business with significant

Howard Marshall & David Grove.

operations in France and, through V&S Galvanizing, the USA. The fit with the group's existing businesses was clear.

The third leg – Industrial Products – was, aside from the growing pipe supports business, largely made up of legacy businesses, some of which harked back to the Hill & Smith of half a century earlier (stampings, pressings, and steel stockholding amongst them), and others representing the rump of Ash & Lacy. Much of this was increasingly viewed as non-core although tactical acquisitions, such as that of Lionweld Kennedy in 2004, were made where they strengthened what already existed.

Grove was described by a close associate as:

"A plain speaker who focussed above all on nurturing management and encouraging sustainable growth over the long-term".

Amongst those he nurtured was Derek Muir, who joined Hill & Smith in 1988, aged 28, as a sales engineer, before progressing to lead first Asset International, and subsequently the core Infrastructure Products Group division. It was Muir who, in 1999, had spotted the potential of Varioguard and sold the opportunity to a very receptive Grove who was keen to see greater energy around product innovation within the group.

So, when Grove stepped away from the Chief Executive role to become Chairman in 2006, Muir was his natural successor and it was he who led the group onto its next chapter, building on the entrepreneurial culture that Grove had embedded across the organisation. They were a successful double-act for three years, before Grove handed over the chair to Bill Whiteley, a well-regarded figure in the industrials sector, and retired from the business altogether in 2009. That same year he was awarded an Order of the British Empire (OBE) for Services to Business in the Queen's Birthday Honours. When David Grove joined, the loss-making Hill & Smith had a market capitalisation of £22m. On his retirement it was valued at £262m and making annual profits of close to £50m.

Building out

If David Grove's period as Chief Executive could be characterised by a fundamental restructuring alongside two transformational deals – Ash & Lacy and Zinkinvent – Derek Muir's time saw the substantial evolution of Hill & Smith into a truly international business.

The group had already dipped its toes into overseas waters – in the USA, France, and Thailand – but when he took over the role in 2006, non-UK sales were less than 10%. When he stepped down in 2020, that figure was over 50%, with over £270m of sales in the USA.

Part of the rationale for overseas expansion lay in what had become an over-reliance on UK government spending. As Muir explained to the *Financial Times* in 2013:

> *"Our percentage of revenues that came from government spending were 24% in 2009, and last year that came down to 11%. We knew that UK government spending was coming down, so we had to find more overseas activities to grow our earnings".*

Having spent eighteen years in the David Grove school of management, it was unsurprising that Muir continued to insist on a decentralised, highly entrepreneurial culture, with management teams across the group encouraged to focus above all on product innovation, whilst the Board concentrated on active portfolio management, selective bolt-on acquisitions, and maximising shareholder returns.

Following the acquisition, in 2007 and 2008, of the remaining 67% of Zinkinvent and the resultant increased scale of the galvanizing business, Hill &

Smith was reorganised into three business segments – Infrastructure Products (35% of sales), Galvanizing Services (28%) and Building & Construction Products (37%). Three years later, with the exit from almost all of the remaining non-core Building & Construction businesses, the group was to focus wholly on Infrastructure Products and Galvanizing Services.

Muir's engineering background gave him a natural flair for product development and one of his great strengths was his close, hands-on engagement with the management teams across the group, encouraging them to generate product ideas. This focus on innovation was central to his organic growth ambitions. As he put it:

"David [Grove] was the strategy man. I was all about building the businesses".

One of his early strategic bets was on the composites market, with the £13m acquisition in 2008 of Creative Pultrusions Inc., increasing the group's presence in the USA and complementing its existing, albeit nascent, interest in fibre reinforced polymer (FRP) products, or composites. Composite products, being lightweight, high strength, corrosion resistant, quick to install and inherently safer in many environments, would become an important, highly profitable driver of growth. A series of complementary US acquisitions followed including Kenway Composites and Tower Tech both in 2017, and Composite Advantage in 2018, so creating a substantial, standalone composites grouping.

The group's strategy in utilities, within its Infrastructure Products division, focused on power markets in emerging economies and on power infrastructure replacement in the developed economies of Europe and the US. With that in mind, Hill & Smith made its then third largest acquisition in 2011 with the £29m purchase of the Paterson Group, a US pipe supports business. Hill & Smith had been in pipe supports – serving the petrochemical, LNG and power generation sectors – in a modest way for some 18 years. However, alongside the group's then existing presence in the UK, Thailand and China, this deal created a global leader and, through its Bergen Pipe Supports business, took Hill & Smith into the nuclear sector for the first time.

It would be harsh to blame the Board for what came next. Just 48 hours after the deal closed, one of the world's worst ever nuclear accidents occurred at the

Fukushima nuclear power station in Japan. The world's nuclear construction industry was in turmoil and would take years to fully recover. Despite this setback, Paterson's US operations would drive the group's pipe supports business in the years that followed. In 2015, the remaining operations in the UK and Thailand were closed with the volumes being transferred to its newly constructed facility in India, now branded Bergen Pipe Supports.

Whilst a series of UK deals had also been done, it was no accident that the largest ones were overseas. As Muir explained at the time:

"The majority of our acquisitions are likely to be privately owned. We also look at distressed businesses in the UK which complement our existing operations and enable us to consolidate our market position. Overseas acquisitions however must have a high-quality management team and a proven earnings stream as it is more demanding to manage businesses from a distance effectively".

In the meantime, elsewhere in Infrastructure Products, business continued to grow across a variety of markets such as the water industry and housebuilding, but it was the longstanding roads business that saw the most significant strategic progress. Muir loved the business. As the *FT* reported in 2013:

"Derek Muir gets a kick out of driving through roadworks. During a 20-minute trip through Birmingham's M6 motorway upgrade, he happily identifies an array of crash barriers, gantries and variable speed limit signs supplied by his company. 'I'm a big fan of roadworks, I love driving through them. That's our barrier there', he says with almost fatherly pride. 'And there is where someone has run into it. And there again…'".

The development of the Varioguard temporary crash barrier rental business had put Hill & Smith firmly on the map in terms of the UK's highways programmes, and the Board was determined to diversify into other markets where road safety was being prioritised through regulation. During 2011 and 2012 some of the group's key roads products, most notably ZoneGuard – an adapted steel temporary barrier system – were launched in the USA, Scandinavia and Australia. The move into Scandinavia was bolstered by the 2011 acquisition of

ZoneGuard, Taunton, Creech Castle.

ATA in Sweden, a supplier of road safety barriers and road signage which subsequently expanded into Norway, and by other smaller deals thereafter. There were further additions to the international roads business in the years that followed including, most notably in terms of scale, the $42m acquisition of Work Area Protection Corp. in the US in 2018.

Hill & Smith was also intent on developing a range of security products such as hostile vehicle mitigation and perimeter security solutions, bollards, barriers and gates. Heightened terror threats were driving demand for protection systems for people, buildings, infrastructure and other areas at risk of attack. By 2020, following the acquisitions of ATG Access and Parking Facilities, all these security-focused businesses had been brought together to create a more substantial platform from which to go after the high growth international security products market.

Another key plank of the growth strategy was to strengthen the position of the galvanizing operations in its core markets, through bolt-on acquisitions in the

UK to consolidate the market and improve the group's footprint, and greenfield developments in the USA in order to create broader geographic coverage based on large, state-of-the-art and therefore highly efficient facilities. By 2020, there were 10 sites in the UK, eight in the USA and 10 in France.

It is fair to say that, after 32 years with Hill & Smith, Muir's final year at the helm was not how he would have scripted it – dominated as it was by the global COVID pandemic. As someone who placed great value on visible leadership and hands-on engagement with his colleagues around the world, the restrictions imposed on normal business frustrated him greatly. That said, Hill & Smith's financial performance was robust, helped by Governments pouring money into infrastructure projects to support their economies. It was really only the Security operations that suffered unduly, due to an almost total lack of mass-participation events for which many of their projects were designed.

Overall, when he stepped down at the end of 2020, Muir left Hill & Smith a very different looking business to when he took over. Within Infrastructure Products, the roads business had broadened out in terms of product range and geography, a niche security business had been developed alongside it, a significant composites business had been created through acquisition, and the purchase of the Paterson Group had enabled the transformation of the pipe supports operation. And, in Galvanizing Services, V&S Galvanizing now comprised a substantial and strategically located network of plants across the USA. Over his tenure, the share price had risen more than fourfold, and the group now had a market value in excess of £1bn.

Turning 200

Towards the end of 2019, as Hill & Smith was nearing its 200th birthday, the role of Chair had passed from Jock Lennox, previously Senior Audit Partner at Ernst & Young (now EY), to Alan Giddins. Having recently stepped down as a Managing Partner and Global Head of Private Equity at 3i Group plc, the FTSE 100 investment company, he brought extensive experience of building businesses in the UK and internationally. Supported initially by Paul Simmons in the role of Chief Executive, Giddins took on the role of Executive Chair in July 2022, on Simmons' departure. The group had also recruited Hannah Nichols as Chief Financial Officer, joining in 2019 from BT, where she had been working in Singapore.

As is often the way when leadership changes, it was an opportunity to take a fresh and dispassionate look at the group's portfolio and assess the strategic priorities for the next chapter. Given his background, it is no surprise that Giddins' early focus was on acquisition strategy, portfolio management, and creating the conditions for the next phase of growth. Part of this was about products and market, and part about people.

In 2022 the major step was taken to sell the galvanizing business in France. The French market had become extremely competitive in recent years and the business was simply not generating the returns that would justify its retention. Alongside this, and for similar reasons, came the exit from the Scandinavian roads business.

Balancing this were a number of important strategic acquisitions. At the end of 2022 Hill & Smith bought National Signal, a US market leader in off-grid solar lighting, and Widnes Galvanising in the UK. These deals were followed in 2023

Lake Tahoe pedestrian footbridge.

and early 2024 by the acquisitions, all in the US, of Enduro Composites, United Fiberglass of America, Korns Galvanizing, Capital Steel and FM Stainless. In aggregate over £85m had been invested over an eighteen month period. One can sense that David Grove would have fully approved of the new energy and drive that had returned to the group's acquisition strategy.

Given the scale of the group and the ambition for further growth both organically and via acquisition, as well as the ever more complex demands of business stewardship, new management structures have been put in place to provide more depth and scalability. This has involved the creation of the new role of Chief Operating Officer, filled by Hooman Caman Javvi, a new Executive Board and, with it, the introduction of Group Presidents into whom the operating companies report. For the first time there have been appointed heads of Health & Safety in both the UK and US, a Group Head of IT and a Group Head of Sustainability. Sustainability has long been a structural growth driver for Hill & Smith – its products and services make infrastructure more sustainable and increase transport safety – and its strategy sets out the target to be net-zero for direct scope greenhouse gas emissions by 2040. Having applied to be a signatory to the Science Based Targets initiative 'Business Ambition to 1.5°C', its targets received approval at the end of 2023.

Hill & Smith therefore enters its third century firing on all cylinders, generating record sales and profits, delivering strong margins and geared up for growth. A leading international provider of sustainable infrastructure products and services, valued at close to £1.5bn and with sales of over £800m, it employs more than 4,250 people worldwide, the majority in its autonomous and agile businesses in the US, UK and India. The owners of the business are major international fund managers, insurance companies and pension funds.

Today, the group is organised into three main divisions:

- Galvanizing Services, increasing the sustainability and maintenance-free life of products including structural steel work, lighting, bridges and other products for industrial and infrastructure markets;
- Engineered Solutions, supplying engineered steel and composite solutions for a wide range of infrastructure markets including power generation and distribution, marine, rail and housing; and engineered pipe supports for the water, power and liquid natural gas markets and for seismic protection solutions;
- Roads & Security, supplying products and services to support road and highway infrastructure including temporary and permanent road safety barriers, intelligent traffic solutions, street lighting columns and bridge parapets; off-grid solar lighting and power solutions; and security products including hostile vehicle mitigation solutions, automated gates and high-security fencing.

From its beginnings as one smoking ironworks in the UK's Black Country, the business has inevitably transformed, and it is tempting to say 'beyond recognition'. But look carefully amongst its operations today, and the way it goes about its business, and it is striking how many of the qualities of the earlier Hill & Smith have endured. Edward Hill and Henry Smith would surely look on with pride at what has been created in their names.

Kylesku Bridge, Scotland.

Part 2:
Hill & Smith Today

Joseph Ash Galvanizing

Founded in 1857 as Joseph Ash & Son, the company grew in tandem with the UK railway industry and became a major supplier to the Great Western Railway Company, which used Joseph Ash extensively for many of its trackside requirements. In 1864 the business joined forces with John Pierce Lacy, which provided galvanizing services, to become Ash & Lacy.

Hill & Smith had had an interest in galvanizing since the middle of the 19th century, but it was the addition of Joseph Ash in 2000, via the takeover of Ash & Lacy plc, that created the critical mass for what is today one of the UK's leading galvanizing businesses.

Joseph Ash Galvanizing.

Pickling items in diluted hydrochloric acid, ready to be hand dipped and spun.

GALVANIZING SERVICES

Hot galvanizing – double dipping a 45ft column.

Skimming or paddling the zinc bath at Joseph Ash Galvanizing.

Joseph Ash Galvanizing

Galvanised steel at Joseph Ash Galvanizing, Walsall.

Headquartered in the West Midlands, Joseph Ash Galvanizing provides a broad range of galvanizing and related steel protection services, including hot dip galvanizing, powder coating, shot blasting and spin galvanizing services. It also offers additional services including collection and delivery, on-site storage facilities, technical support, and assistance with the bundling, packing, and labelling of steel.

With the acquisitions of Medway Galvanizing in 2013, Premier Galvanizing in 2015 and Widnes Galvanising in 2022, Joseph Ash now has a network of nine strategically located sites across the UK – in Bilston, Bridgend, Chesterfield, Corby, Hull, Medway, Telford, Walsall and Widnes. Through these, it serves the construction, infrastructure, agriculture, transport, energy, telecoms and datacentre sectors, as well as more traditional customers such as architects and sculptors.

The Telford site has one of the widest galvanizing baths in Europe, and the Chesterfield site has the second-longest bath in the UK at over 16 metres. The Chesterfield site was also the first galvanizing facility in the UK to be awarded Fit for Nuclear status – reserved only for companies that meet the strict requirements of the nuclear sector.

V&S Galvanizing

The foundations of V&S Galvanizing were laid in 1985 when Voigt & Schweitzer purchased its first US plant, in Columbus, Ohio in 1985.

The business then grew through the acquisition of galvanizing businesses in Detroit and Philadelphia together with greenfield developments in Massachusetts,

Columbus plant.

V&S Galvanizing

Harrisburg International Airport.

Galvanizing bath.

New Jersey and Pennsylvania, until it became part of Hill & Smith as a result of the group's acquisition of Zinkinvent, completed in 2008. This provided the platform for further growth of the group's US galvanizing operations.

V&S Galvanizing's hot-dip galvanizing process involves the immersion of fabricated steel into a bath of molten zinc at a temperature of c.840°F, to provide a corrosion resistant coating on

Freedom Tower, NY.

the steel's surface, dramatically increasing its sustainability and maintenance-free life. Its V&S COLORZINQ duplex system, which combines zinc coating with paint applied by its expert technicians, has been found to offer greater protection against corrosion over paint with no galvanization. It can dip a range of materials, at all sizes from a small hex-cap screw in one of the centrifuges, to a 90 foot I-Beam in its largest kettle.

V&S Galvanizing provides these services for a wide range of applications in the industrial and infrastructure markets such as bridges, highways, utilities, solar, architectural, energy, vehicles and transportation, agricultural equipment, oil and gas, chemicals and construction. High profile projects over the years include the West 57th St Pyramid Building, New York City; the Mount Olive Solar Farm, New Jersey; the Tappan Zee Bridge, New York; the Riviere Cochon Gras Bridge, Haiti and the Freedom Tower, New York.

Still headquartered in Ohio, V&S Galvanizing has steadily developed its presence, through a combination of acquisition and greenfield developments, to create a network of large, state-of-the-art and highly efficient facilities. It now has nine strategically located facilities in Ohio, Delaware, Massachusetts, Michigan, New Jersey, New York, Pennsylvania and Tennessee, serving customers across the Northeastern USA.

Bergen Pipe Supports

With roots stretching back to the 1950s, Bergen Pipe Supports designs and manufactures solutions to support piping, vessels and equipment used in energy industries worldwide.

Its products are designed for use in very harsh environments, operating at temperatures from as low as -196°C up to 850°C. They include engineered pipe hangers, restraints and composite materials, including constant and variable effort supports, hydraulic snubbers, thermal insulation and isolation.

Sri City, India.

Bergen Pipe Supports

With manufacturing and quality control systems that have been developed over many years, the business is able to design optimum solutions for its customers' unique requirements.

It works extensively with global engineering, procurement, and construction (EPC) contractors, supplying to most facets of the energy industry: the extraction, storage and transportation of liquified natural gas (LNG); petrochemical complexes; oil and gas production and processing plants; and renewable energy, fertilizer production, biomass energy and wastewater treatment.

Cryogenic shoe for 80" pipe supplied to LNG project.

The business has a Global Purchasing Agreement with a major EPC in Japan and Europe for its power generation plants, and has recently supplied pre-insulated, cryogenic pipe supports for major LNG terminals worldwide.

Its factory in the south of Andhra Pradesh, just north of Chennai, was purpose-built in 2012 and, following the reorganisation of Hill & Smith's non-US pipe supports businesses in 2016, became a centre of excellence for the group. As part of its ongoing product development initiatives, Bergen Pipe Supports is creating new opportunities for engineered composites for use in wastewater treatment plants, large storage tanks and sustainable transport applications.

Bergatherm composites.

Birtley Group

The business began trading in 1965 as Birtley Lintels, a manufacturer of steel lintels for the UK's booming housebuilding industry, and was acquired by Hill & Smith in 1981.

1996 saw the addition of a galvanizing facility, and Birtley's capabilities were further expanded through the acquisitions of Expamet in 2012, and Bowater Doors in 2015.

Birtley Group

Bowater Doors.

Based in County Durham, UK, Birtley Group today manufactures and supplies bespoke steel products and services for the housebuilding and construction industries, including lintels, doors and materials, delivered through a network of builders' merchants and distributors across the UK. A research and development programme has seen the launch of several new products and sustainability-led solutions to meet the evolving needs of its end users.

Birtley produces standard and bespoke lintels, including Supatherm, a range of thermally broken lintels designed to cause a dramatic reduction in heat loss and meet revised Part L building regulations. Birtley's lintels are the only UK line to be galvanized following fabrication.

Bowater Doors manufactures composite and fire doors for residential new builds as well as renovation projects for social housing houses, flats, and tower blocks. Its products deliver robust construction, outstanding energy-efficient performance, low maintenance and high security.

Expamet fabricates over 7,000 tons of pre-galvanized and stainless steel products, and some 40 million metres of plasterers' accessories, each year.

Birtley Group – galvanizing.

ENGINEERED SOLUTIONS

Expamet coils.

More recently, the Group launched Birtley Masonry Supports to promote bespoke windpost, masonry support and brick slip lintel products.

Alongside these brands, Birtley Galvanizing provides a state-of-the-art hot-dip galvanizing facility for customers ranging from artists to street furniture manufacturers, and for high profile projects such as the entrance gates to the Poison Garden at Northumberland's Alnwick Gardens.

Creative Composites Group

Creative Composites Group (CCG) traces its roots back to the formation of Creative Pultrusions in 1973. Creative Pultrusions was acquired by Hill & Smith in 2008.

Now made up of multiple companies – Creative Pultrusions, Kenway Composites, Tower Tech, Composite Advantage, Enduro Composites and United Fiberglass – CCG provides a wide array of composite products for industrial and infrastructure applications. Services include comprehensive engineering, design and consultation, building and fabrication services, field services and repairs.

Advanced structural composites take the world's infrastructure beyond the limitations of traditional concrete, steel and wood. CCG offers technical innovation

Original Creative Pultrusion manufacturing building.

Firestrong FRP pole.

Creative Composites Group

West Thames pedestrian bridge deck, Lower Manhattan, NYC.

Rail Platform Chelsea, Ma-10 2.

Yellow Creek pedestrian bridge.

backed by the industry's most vertically integrated manufacturing capability. As a result of the 2023 acquisitions of Enduro Composites and United Fiberglass, CCG now covers every manufacturing process for structural Fibre Reinforced Polymer (FRP) composites.

Headquartered in Pennsylvania and with operations across the US, CCG is an innovative group serving industries including utilities and telecommunications, building products, mass transit, marine, pulp and paper, bridge construction, and conduit and cable management. Products include utility poles and crossarms, bridge decking and drainage systems, rail platforms and access structures, waterfront pipe and sheet piles, cooling towers, industrial tanks, cable management systems, water and wastewater systems, building panels and trusses. These are engineered to perform in the most challenging environments with excellent corrosion resistance, high strength-to-weight ratio, Shieldstrong™ UV protection, StormStrong® weather protection, FireStrong™ fire protection and environmental sustainability.

Lionweld Kennedy

Lionweld Kennedy Group's origins lie as far back as 1910, with the formation of PA Mudd & Company, one of the first electric arc welding companies in the UK.

Lionweld Steel Flooring and Stairway Co. stand.

Welding at Lionweld Kennedy.

Towards the end of the 1920s Lionweld Steel Flooring and Stairway Company was formed, manufacturing open steel flooring and stair treads in a diamond pattern, using a method of resistance welding developed by PA Mudd.

Lionweld Steel Flooring and Stairway merged with Allan Kennedy & Co. in 1988 to create Lionweld Kennedy, then the largest manufacturer of open mesh steel grating in the UK. Lionweld Kennedy was then acquired by Hill & Smith in 2004 and, in 2010, it added Redman Fisher, a market leader in Ireland supplying Flowforge steel grating and handrailing systems.

Based in Middlesborough and with three sites in the UK and Ireland, the business now designs, manufactures and installs industrial access products including open mesh flooring, stair treads, handrail, gates and ladders, in both steel and GRP. Its products are used in the renewable energy sector (particularly offshore wind), and in the data centre, utilities and construction industries across the UK and Europe. Its open mesh flooring is fully compliant to both British and European Standards and is the established industry standard, to the extent that in many sectors, the oil and gas industry in particular, such flooring is known simply as 'Kennedy Grating'.

Lionweld Kennedy is working in collaboration with business partners to remove embedded carbon from its industry and is committed to being a Carbon Net Zero organisation (scopes 1 & 2) by 2040. Through its Carbon Reduction Plan, it has already reduced its annual carbon emissions by 76%.

Novia Corporation

Novia Corporation provides vibration isolation and seismic restraint engineering services and custom manufactured equipment for the commercial construction and heating, ventilation, and air conditioning (HVAC) markets. The business was founded in 1990 and acquired by Hill & Smith in 2015. It is headquartered in New Hampshire, USA.

Novia Headquarters, New Hampshire, USA.

Seismic and vibration isolation adapter curb at Yale University.

Mocked up modular seismic and vibration isolation curb in Novia's shop.

Novia's business is built on technical expertise, customer service and quality. Its products and engineering services provide solutions to vibration concerns, seismic restraint needs, thermal expansion and contraction issues, challenging acoustic applications, and the prevention of excessive movement in plumbing and HVAC equipment.

Products include roof curbs, flashable rails, equipment supports, inertia bases, catwalks, service platforms, stair systems, structural steel support systems, cooling tower rails, spring hangers and mounts, all custom designed and manufactured in Novia's recently renovated and expanded production facility. End-users include mechanical and general contractors, original equipment manufacturers, and building owners in the commercial, industrial, institutional and healthcare construction markets.

Much of its business is driven by the International Building Code (IBC), wind and seismic codes and project specifications. Specifying mechanical and structural engineers, tasked with determining materials, products and construction methods, often direct project executives to Novia.

New England is Novia's largest market but the business also supports customers throughout the US and southern Canada. The 2023 acquisition of ConnFab, a New England-based curb and rail manufacturer, has further increased its product range and geographic reach.

One section of a large modular seismic curb at Mount Sinai Hospital in New York City.

The Paterson Group

Founded in 1908 to supply the nascent plumbing industry, the Paterson Group today supplies engineered support systems for all types of piping in commercial and industrial infrastructure installations. It was acquired by Hill & Smith in 2011.

Headquartered in Louisiana, USA, and co-branded as Carpenter & Paterson and Bergen Pipe Supports, the group supplies customers throughout the US from its facilities in Louisiana, Massachusetts, New Jersey, Pennsylvania, California and, as of early 2024 following the group's acquisition of FM Stainless, Georgia.

Its pipe support systems are engineered to handle the extreme environments in which they operate, managing critical factors such as stress loads on bridges, highly corrosive environments including chemical and water treatment plants, and temperature changes in power plants ranging from -200°C to +1,000°C.

The business was a leading supplier in the construction of the United States' nuclear power fleet in the US in the 1970s and 1980s and continues to supply both commercial and military nuclear applications.

Its products and engineering services are now specified in vital infrastructure including hospitals, water treatment, power generation, military, roads and bridges, chemical plants, sports stadiums, universities and airports. It is a major supplier to environmentally-friendly sectors such as electric vehicle and battery manufacture, the supply of clean safe drinking water, and hydrogen power generation plants.

Carpenter & Paterson operates a commercial catalogue hardware business from five distribution facilities across the US, with an inventory of over 33,000 different stock items.

The Paterson Group is currently investing to modernise and double its manufacturing capabilities in Louisiana and Pennsylvania, to include advanced robotics, CNC machining, and automated metal fabrication, not only improving quality and delivery for customers, but also significantly improving safety for its employees.

V&S Schuler Utilities Group

Founded in 1939, the Charles E Schuler Company played an integral role in the development of the United States' power grid, fabricating structural steel for the emerging electrical utility industry. The company was acquired by Voigt & Schweitzer in 1991 and then, as V&S Schuler, became part of Hill & Smith when the group acquired Zinkinvent in 2008.

Still headquartered in Ohio, US, V&S Schuler has steadily expanded its footprint and manufacturing capacity, acquiring an Ohio fabrication business in 2018 and, most recently, a New Jersey fabrication business in early 2024.

Burton, Ohio plant.

Electric substation, USA.

ENGINEERED SOLUTIONS

Laser cutting technology. *Welder at Ohio plant.*

As a result, V&S Schuler Utilities today consists of four companies – V&S Schuler Engineering and V&S Schuler Packaging in Ohio, V&S Tubular Products in Oklahoma, and V&S Capital Steel in New Jersey – that fabricate steel and supply other products and services to the electrical utility market, rural electrical co-operatives and manufacturing industries across the US. Management at each of these facilities continuously looks for ways to make improvements that ensure V&S Schuler meets the highest standards.

Tubular steel section for the transmission and distribution sector.

Substation, USA.

Together, these companies can provide all the material for substations, transmission and distribution lines, and numerous other structures. They fabricate structural steel and aluminium for substation construction, lattice towers and tapered tubular poles for transmission and distribution, and supply comprehensive structure and component packages, enabling customers to complete their projects in the fastest, most convenient, and cost-effective way possible. V&S Schuler also fabricates steels for bridges, buildings, stadiums, conveyor systems, concrete imbeds, and special bespoke projects.

Based on drawings and customer criteria, skilled programmers create exact programs for each piece of material. State-of-the-art equipment is then used to punch, drill, shear and cut the material precisely to customers' specifications.

In addition, V&S Schuler has the capability to design structures and associated foundations, provide electrical high-voltage design and furnish associated electrical arrangement drawings.

ATG Access

Founded in 1989, ATG Access is headquartered in Merseyside, UK, and manufactures in the UK, USA, Singapore and the United Arab Emirates.

The business designs, manufactures, installs and services intelligent, physical security solutions such as bollards, road blockers, barriers and gates to protect critical national infrastructure and sensitive sites from hostile vehicles, vehicles as weapons of terrorism, and ram-raid attacks in over 40 countries. Its portfolio includes automatic, manually retractable, fixed, removeable and shallow mounted applications, many of which are crash-tested to either PAS 68, IWA-14, ASTM or DOS standards.

It developed the world's first shallow mount foundation bollard with its innovative foundation plate design. This transformed gate and barrier technology with its synthetic fibre system, exploits its ultra-lightweight yet high-strength properties to enable slimmer and more aesthetic protective structures.

Emirates football stadium, Arsenal.

ATG Access

Changi Airport, Singapore.

Alongside this, ATG Access developed the world's highest strength automatic and fixed shallow mount bollard, capable of stopping a 30 tonne vehicle travelling at 80kph. It was the first supplier, and remains one of the few, to gain highways TOPAS approval, enabling it to install protective measures onto public carriageways.

Over the past 34 years ATG Access has become world renowned for its expertise, quality and innovative capabilities, and has delivered projects across the UK, Europe, Scandinavia, the Baltics, Asia, Australia, New Zealand, the Kingdom of Saudi Arabia and the wider GCC region, and the USA.

These projects have included the Hamad International Airport in Qatar, Dubai Airport, the King's Palace in Malaysia, Los Angeles International Airport, Singapore Changi Airport, the Sydney Opera House, the UK's Houses of Parliament and Westminster Bridge, numerous premiership football stadiums, and the 2012 London Olympics.

The business was acquired by Hill & Smith in 2019.

Westminster Bridge.

ROADS & SECURITY

Asset International Structures

Asset International Structures can trace its roots back to 1896, with the creation of Armco Indiana, USA. The company started trading from offices in London in 1924 and constructed its Newport site, named Armco Construction Products Ltd, in 1954. In 1986 the company was sold to Hill & Smith and renamed Asset International Structures.

Armco Multi Plate arch, relining a failing concrete arch bridge.

Armco ingot iron riveted culvert, June 1939.

Based in Cwmbran, South Wales, the business is a leading design and supply consultant for the road, rail, renewables and utilities sectors within the UK and Ireland, as well as internationally. Its innovative products help infrastructure become more sustainable by providing off-site modular construction, minimising embodied carbon and maximising safety.

Its steel range includes Asset MultiPlate®, a construction system based around corrugated, curved and galvanized steel sheets; Asset StrenCor, a versatile deep corrugated structure for the road and rail sectors; and Asset BaFix™, an innovative track ballast

shoulder retention system for the rail industry. Its concrete range includes the Asset BEBO® precast concrete arch system for the design and construction of earth overfilled bridges, tunnels, culverts and green bridges, and the Asset VSoL Retained Earth Wall System, a cost-effective construction technique suitable for a variety of retaining wall applications. Its Asset FRP range consists of composite rail platforms, lightweight bridges, bridge decks and cantilever sidewalks, along with bridge beams which provide strength and stability to bridge structures.

In 2023, Asset International Structures received funding, as a result of a National Highways competition, for the development of an Asset FRP bridge beam with embedded smart monitoring, which reduces full lifecycle costs as well as maintenance visits through access to real-time data. This concept was developed in collaboration with the University of Southampton. The business has also recently been awarded gold status from the Supply Chain Sustainability School.

Barkers Engineering

Based in Staffordshire, UK, Barkers designs and manufactures perimeter security solutions to protect people, property and reputations. Founded in 1861 by Wilfred Barker, the business began life engineering equipment for the mines and coalfields. It was acquired by Hill & Smith in 1968.

Today, Barkers primary business is the manufacture of steel security fencing for commercial customers, but it also has three supporting trading divisions: galvanizing was added in 1991 to meet the demand for its fencing products; a powder coating plant was subsequently added in 2001; followed by Barkers

Barkers Engineering galvanizing bath.

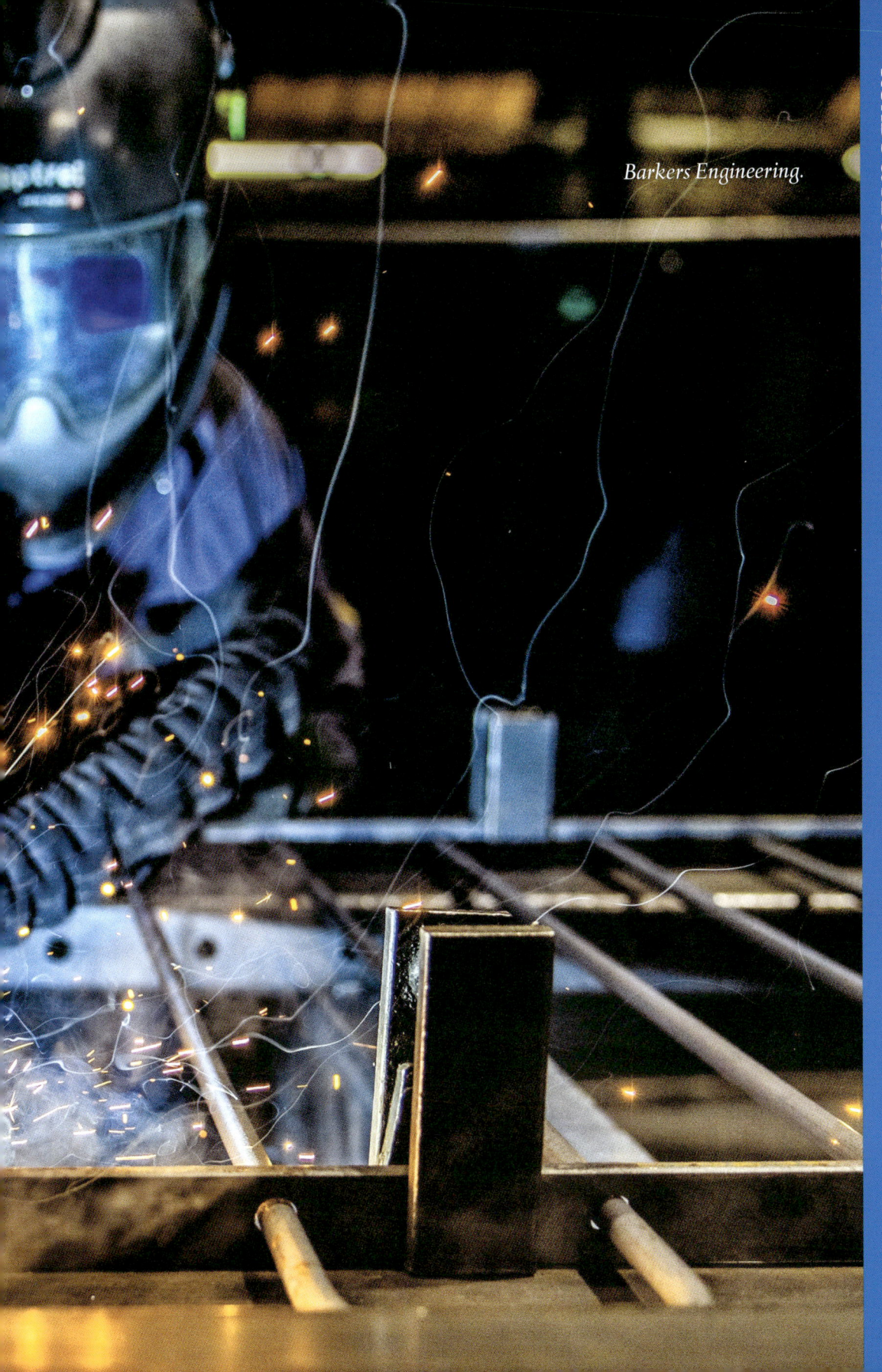

ROADS & SECURITY

Barkers Engineering.

Barkers StronGuard, Papua New Guinea.

Fasteners in 2003. By having its own fabrication, galvanizing and powder coating plants all on the same site, the business can provide a unique level of service, enabling ultimate control over quality and service for external customers and support for other companies within Hill & Smith.

More recently, Barkers has developed a range of high-security fencing and gates that are LPS1175 and NPSA accredited. It also offers a range of palisade and mesh crash fences that are PAS 68 certified to stop a 7.5 tonne truck at 30mph. These high-security and crash-rated fences protect data centres, military sites, critical national infrastructure and other high value sites both in the UK and overseas.

Hill & Smith Inc.

In 2008, Hill & Smith created Hill & Smith Inc. as a new platform from which to expand the reach of its roads and safety operations into the US market.

The first product introduced was ZoneGuard®, a portable steel crash barrier system. Whilst portable steel barriers had been used for decades throughout Europe, this innovative design was new to American highways but, having undergone extensive crash testing to meet the Manual for Assessing Safety Hardware (MASH) requirements, it launched successfully in the US in 2009.

Variable speed limit deployed in Richfield, Ohio 2023.

ROADS & SECURITY

Based in Columbus, Ohio, Hill & Smith Inc. is now an established industry-leading manufacturer of a wide range of transportation safety products. These include temporary steel and concrete crash barrier, impact attenuators, directional trailered products such as arrow and message boards, intelligent transportation solutions such as queue detection systems, egress warning systems, mobile radar, mobile camera, proximity warning systems and HS Connect software.

In 2018 the business acquired Work Area Protection, a large and respected supplier of complementary temporary traffic control devices and innovative safety solutions worldwide.

With several manufacturing locations across the US producing a range of MASH-compliant and Federal Highway Administration-approved technologies, Hill & Smith Inc. is dedicated to making highways and work zones safer for both roadside workers and motorists.

Hill & Smith Infrastructure

Within Hill & Smith Infrastructure is the group's original business, Hill & Smith, founded in 1824.

Having specialised in its early days in puddling machines, ornamental gates, fences and structural steel work, the 1920s marked a turning point with the focus turning to steel railings and bridges, with public safety at the forefront of its

Brierly Hill Factory c.1950.

HVM installation at a Christmas market.

M40/M42 upgrade, temporary steel barrier and pre-cast concrete barrier.

Raha Beach Interchange, Abu Dhabi, bridge parapets.

Permanent steel barriers, A14, Huntington, UK.

work. The business started manufacturing crash barriers for the Department of Transport – the first fully-tested restraint systems on the market – in 1971.

Through four long-established businesses – Asset VRS, Hardstaff Barriers, Hill & Smith Barriers and Varley & Gulliver – Hill & Smith Infrastructure now provides a wide variety of market-leading temporary and permanent vehicle restraint system (VRS) and hostile vehicle mitigation (HVM) solutions.

Products include temporary and permanent steel and concrete road safety barriers and vehicle restraint systems, security and delineation solutions, bridge parapets, pedestrian barriers and security gates. Some of its best-known brands today are ZoneGuard, MASS, Brifen, Bristorm and HiMast.

Still based in the UK's West Midlands, and with a road barrier presence in Australia, Hill & Smith Infrastructure serves a wide range of industries including road, rail and aviation infrastructure, construction and public security, with both private and public sector customers around the world. In recent years, its VRS solutions have been specified and installed on some of the largest UK highway projects and on overseas road networks. Its HVM solutions have been deployed to provide protection and security for a variety of public spaces from music venues to high-profile occasions including royal events.

Mallatite

Mallatite was originally a fencing coating business before moving into lighting column manufacture in 1991. The business was acquired by Hill & Smith in 2002 and its diverse product range was  subsequently enhanced by the acquisitions of Signature in 2016 and Signpost Solutions in 2020. Based in Derbyshire, it operates from five strategically located and fully accredited locations around the UK.

Mallatite is now a leading provider of road and rail infrastructure and traffic management solutions, including lighting and signage, columns, and products to enhance road and pedestrian safety. Recent product additions include signalling equipment for the UK rail network and critical smart solutions using a range of products to capture real-time data from assets and so reduce costs for customers. Its Chesterfield manufacturing site provides an in-house corrosion protection system – Plascoat PPA 571 – a thermoplastic coating that effectively prolongs the lifespan of lighting columns by up to 50 years.

Mallatite vehicle activated sign.

Mallatite wig wag (level crossing) signal.

Chesterfield Plascoat PPA 571 powder coating line.

Mallatite aluminium column.

Mallatite has built a reputation for providing reliable and innovative designs and products to a wide range of industries, in both the private and public sectors. These have been used across the UK roads, motorways and surrounding areas and have supported some key projects in recent years, including the integration of Smart Cities throughout the UK, new signalling for Network Rail including the Birmingham New Street station upgrade, speed reduction projects across Wales, the 2022 Commonwealth Games in Birmingham, and bespoke decorative lighting columns for Ireland's Port Rush Golf Club for its hosting of the 2019 Ryder Cup.

National Signal

Founded in 1997, when it introduced the first membrane LED display arrow control, National Signal is now a market leading manufacturer of solar and solar/diesel hybrid portable light towers, traffic control message signs, and flashing arrow boards. The business was acquired by Hill & Smith in 2022.

Based in southern California, it serves customers principally across the USA, Central America and Australia.

Providing both permanent and temporary lighting solutions, its Solar Light Tower series is its flagship product. Ideal in low-to-no-lighting environments such as in construction, mining and utilities, it can also illuminate streets, car parks, parks, neighbourhoods and other high-traffic areas for safety and security. Its full line of traffic control products includes several sizes of digital message signs, speed trailers, vehicle mounted flashing arrows and illuminated street name signs.

The SunRay LTS solar light tower providing safety at an event.

Using its own LED dimmable drivers that extend the operating time of its towers,

A fleet of solar light towers departing from the manufacturing facility.

National Signal's patented energy saving profile reduces energy consumption to the lowest levels possible. Its patents in energy management include a touch pad control that allows the user to make changes to their tower and get instant feedback on its performance for the entire year. This allows the user to maximize the tower's efficiency.

Its products are now the industry choice for two of the largest national rental companies in the USA.

Parking Facilities

Established in 2000 and based in Staffordshire, Parking Facilities is the UK's leading supply partner for vehicular and pedestrian access management solutions, working with the private, public and charitable sectors.

Rising arm barrier.

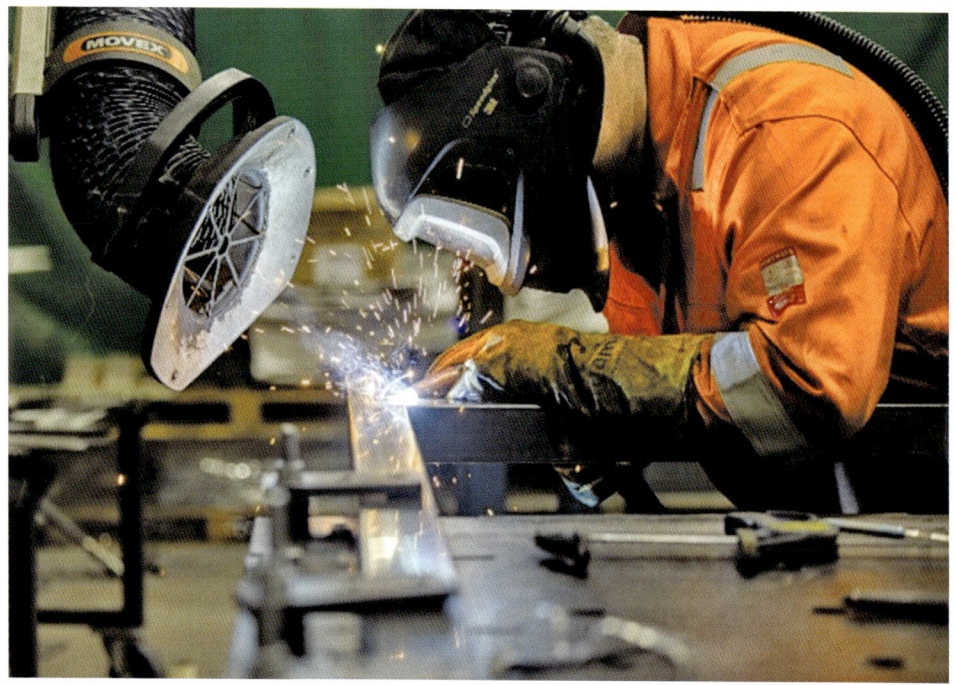

Its range of automatic and manual barriers, turnstiles, bollards, sliding gates, bi-folding gates and swing gates have become the gold standard in the industry due to their simple design, customisability and plug-and-play nature, avoiding over-complicated installation processes.

All its products are manufactured from durable aluminium or galvanized steel, making them resistant to the elements and renowned for their strength. They are created bespoke, based on clients' functional and aesthetic requirements. From initial consultation to design, and manufacture to delivery, Parking Facilities offers complete perimeter access management solutions.

Parking Facilities was acquired by Hill & Smith in 2019. Its range complements the group's other hostile vehicle mitigation (HVM) and related security product offerings, creating a comprehensive range of perimeter security solutions to customers in both the UK and international markets, with the highest standards of security, automation and convenience.

Prolectric

Prolectric has been the UK's leading off-grid, renewable lighting, power and security specialist since it introduced the first all-in-one solar street light to the market in 2011. The business was acquired by Hill & Smith in 2021.

Based in Clevedon, Bristol, and with six sites across the UK, Prolectric's mission is to power the world's off-grid energy needs with smart, clean, renewable technology. Its solar street lights, mobile tower lights and solar-hybrid power products and advanced telematics software provide unparalleled performance, reducing or eliminating carbon emissions, fuel and noise, and saving costs.

Prolight – A14 National Highways project.

Since the 2016 launch of ProLight, its first award-winning mobile solar lighting tower that works autonomously all year round, it is estimated to have already saved 35k tonnes of CO_2 and reduced customers' diesel usage by more than 10 million litres. In 2021, Prolectric received the Queen's Award for Enterprise: Sustainable Development.

Prolectric's solutions, available either to buy or rent, are used on construction, rail and major infrastructure worksites. The company also works with major telecoms and facilities management companies, as well as the UK Government, creating cleaner, quieter and safer working environments.

A6 permanent street light.

ROADS & SECURITY